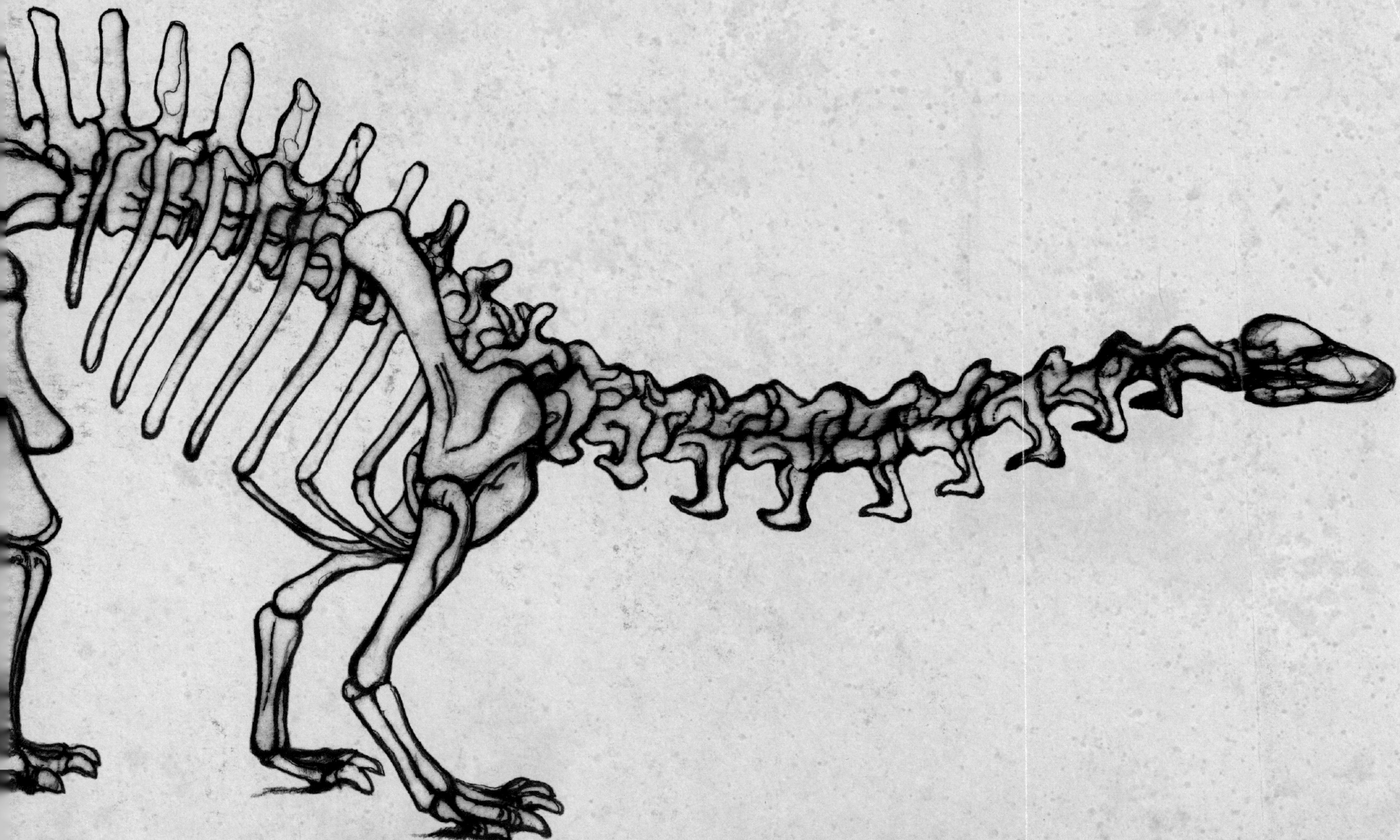

Skeleton of *Apatosaurus excelsus* (*Brontosaurus excelsus*) copied from an 1883 drawing by O. C. Marsh

DINO
MOUN

SAUR
NTAIN

Digging into the Jurassic Age

Deborah Kogan Ray

FRANCES FOSTER BOOKS • FARRAR STRAUS GIROUX • NEW YORK

In 1868, audiences crowded the Academy of Natural Sciences in Philadelphia to see the first dinosaur ever exhibited in America.

William Parker Foulke, an amateur fossil hunter, had discovered the bones used to cast the model ten years earlier, in a marl pit in Haddonfield, New Jersey. Named *Hadrosaurus*—"bulky lizard"—for its shape, it was the first nearly complete dinosaur excavated in the United States.

The directors of the exhibit were Joseph Leidy, the museum's curator, and Edward Drinker Cope, who had worked on the excavation. Both were paleontologists, scientists who study ancient bones and fossils. Their hope was that the display would spark public interest in the still little-known science.

And it did.

Within two years, more than 165,000 people from all over the world came to see the three-story-high skeleton assembled by British sculptor Benjamin Waterhouse Hawkins. Among scientists studying the prehistoric world, fervor to find more dinosaurs in North America triggered what would become known as the "Bone Wars."

For thousands of years, people found the bones of dinosaurs—but no one knew what they were.

In ancient China, they were believed to be dragon bones that possessed magical powers. In medieval Europe, they were imagined to belong to mythical monsters.

In 1842, Sir Richard Owen, a British paleontologist, invented a name to describe what they really were. It is made up of two Greek words—*deinos* and *sauros*—meaning "terrible lizard."

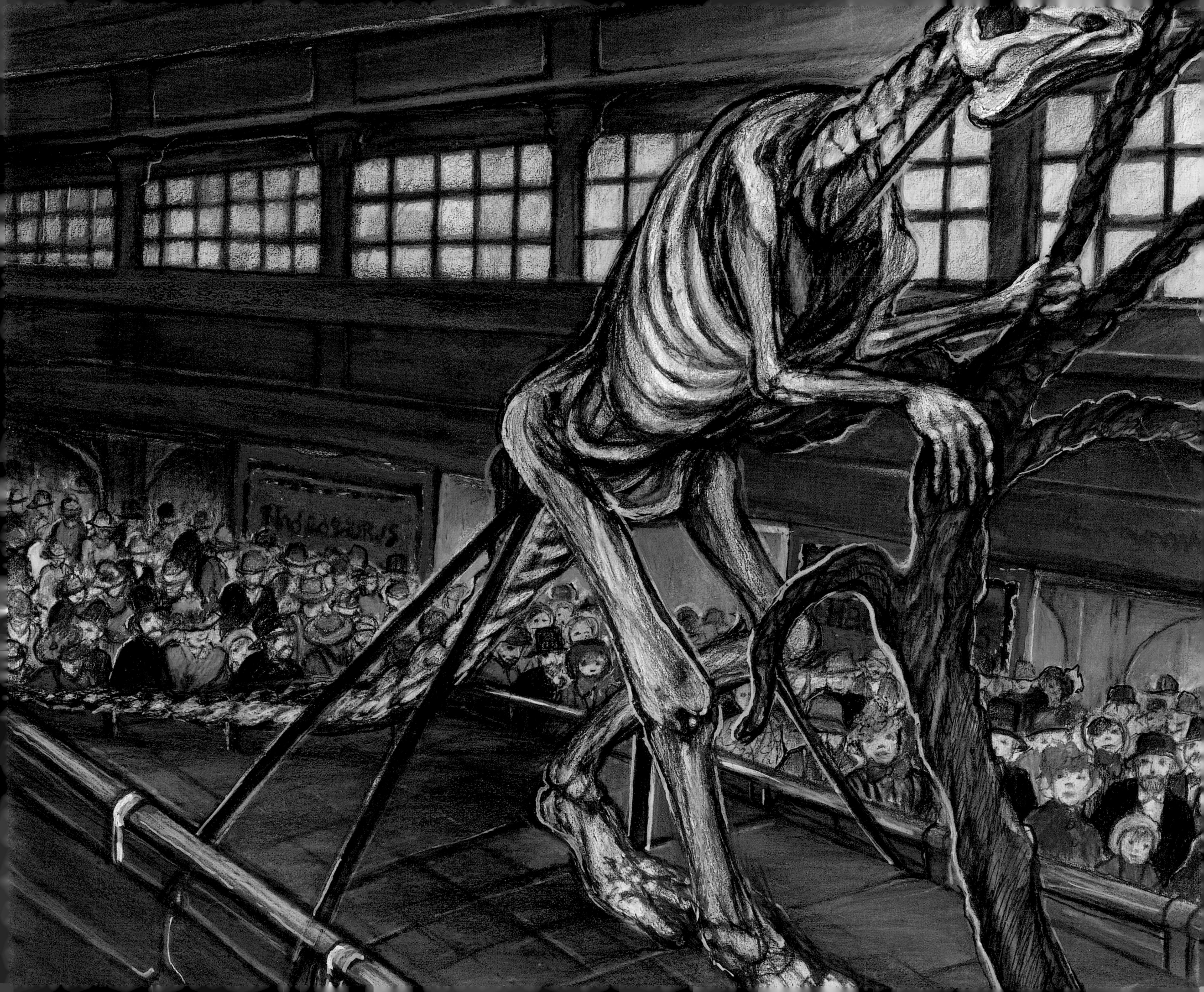

The dinosaur rush took off in 1877, when huge dinosaur bones were discovered in Morrison, Colorado, a small mining town west of Denver. Soon after, bones were discovered in the Garden Park area, near Cañon City, Colorado. Another discovery quickly followed at Como Bluff, Wyoming.

The news traveled fast. "Bone hunters"—as paleontologists had been nicknamed by the public—headed west in hopes of finding a treasure trove of new dinosaurs.

The Bone Wars continued for more than twenty years, fueled by a fierce rivalry between two of the country's most famous paleontologists—Edward Drinker Cope and Othniel Charles Marsh, curator at the Peabody Museum of Natural History in New Haven, Connecticut.

In their quest for glory, both men rushed to find and describe the greatest number of prehistoric creatures and to claim scientific credit for their discoveries. Their achievements were extraordinary. Cope classified and named fifty-six different species of dinosaurs, and Marsh is credited with eighty-six.

But competition between the two men was so bitter that the rivals are said to have stooped to underhanded methods, including spying, bribery, and even hijacking fossil shipments bound back east for each other's museums.

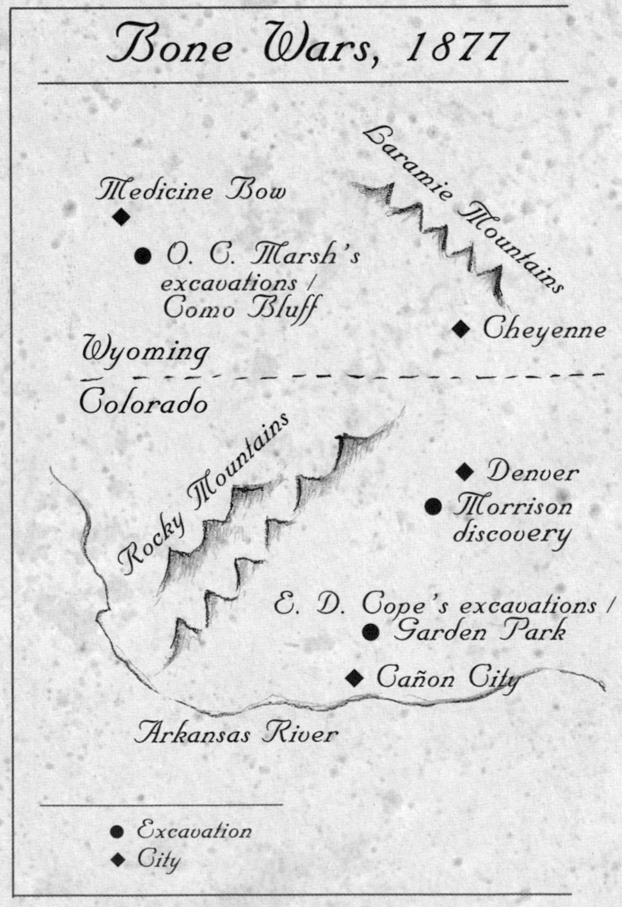

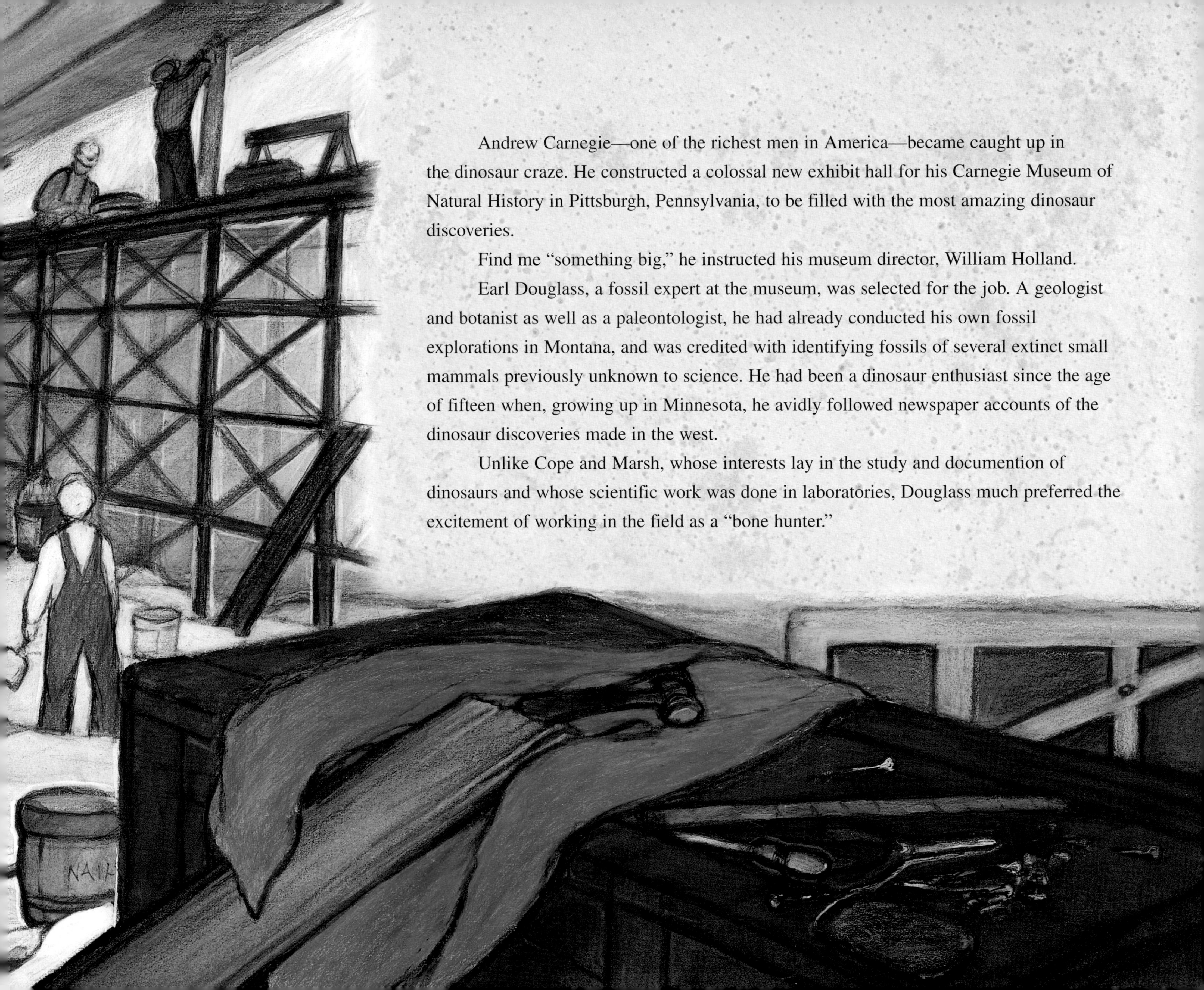

Andrew Carnegie—one of the richest men in America—became caught up in the dinosaur craze. He constructed a colossal new exhibit hall for his Carnegie Museum of Natural History in Pittsburgh, Pennsylvania, to be filled with the most amazing dinosaur discoveries.

Find me "something big," he instructed his museum director, William Holland.

Earl Douglass, a fossil expert at the museum, was selected for the job. A geologist and botanist as well as a paleontologist, he had already conducted his own fossil explorations in Montana, and was credited with identifying fossils of several extinct small mammals previously unknown to science. He had been a dinosaur enthusiast since the age of fifteen when, growing up in Minnesota, he avidly followed newspaper accounts of the dinosaur discoveries made in the west.

Unlike Cope and Marsh, whose interests lay in the study and documention of dinosaurs and whose scientific work was done in laboratories, Douglass much preferred the excitement of working in the field as a "bone hunter."

Though Earl Douglass had no interest in glory, the opportunity to conduct an expedition in search of "something big" was a dream come true.

He immediately began to study topographic maps and geologic surveys of the entire Morrison Formation—a group of rock layers named for the town where the first dinosaur discoveries of the Bone Wars were made. A vast area that originated as floodplain deposits about 150 million years ago, during the Jurassic period, the Morrison Formation covers much of the American west. From the Dakotas, Nebraska, and Kansas in the east, it stretches to include nearly all of Colorado and Wyoming, eastern Utah and Idaho, and most of Montana, as well as, to the south, a corner of Arizona, northern New Mexico, and the tip of the panhandle of Oklahoma.

The most extensive and abundant dinosaur excavations had been done in Colorado and Wyoming. But Douglass, guided by instinct and his knowledge of rock strata, believed that the vast untouched areas in northeastern Utah held the greatest potential for finding Jurassic dinosaurs.

In the spring of 1908, he set out for the Uinta Basin, where he spent the summer exploring near the Green River. By late September, he had amassed a collection of small mammal and reptile fossils to send back to the museum.

But he had found nothing big.

Unio (clam)
These fossils are prevalent in the strata of sedimentary Jurassic sandstone of the Uinta area.

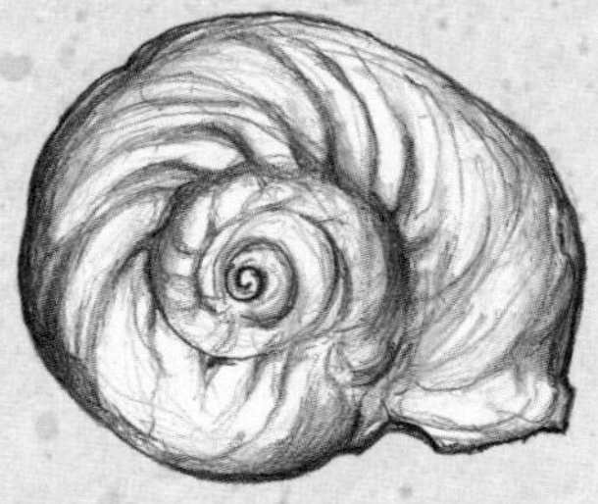

Ammonite
Extinct marine animals that are related to modern squid, octopus, and chambered nautilus.

Crocodile teeth
Crocodiles have remained unchanged since the age of dinosaurs.

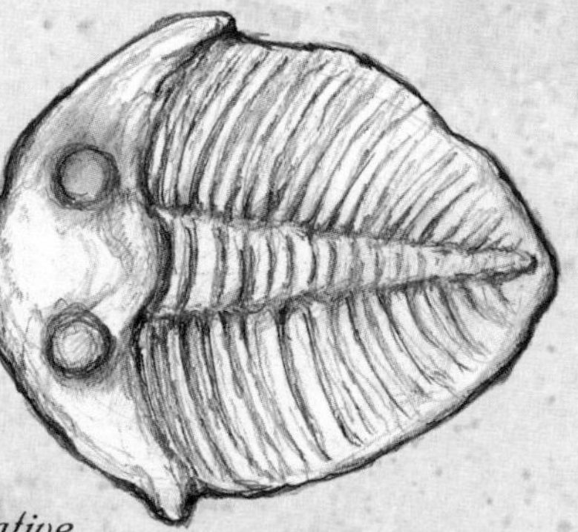

Trilobite
An evolutionary relative of the spider, they ranged in size from 1 millimeter to 2 feet long!

Knightia
A common fossil fish found in layers of limestone in the Green River Formation.

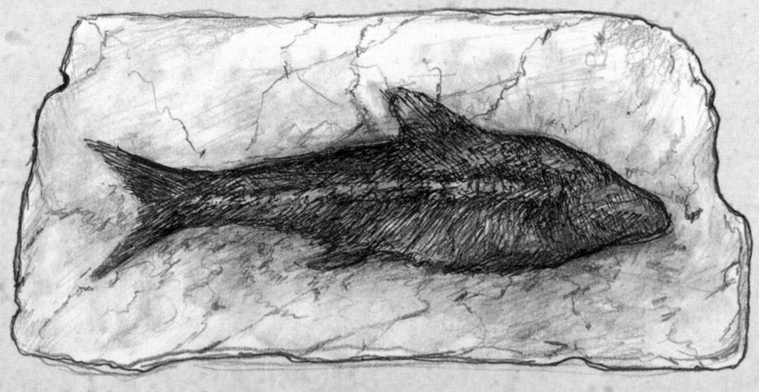

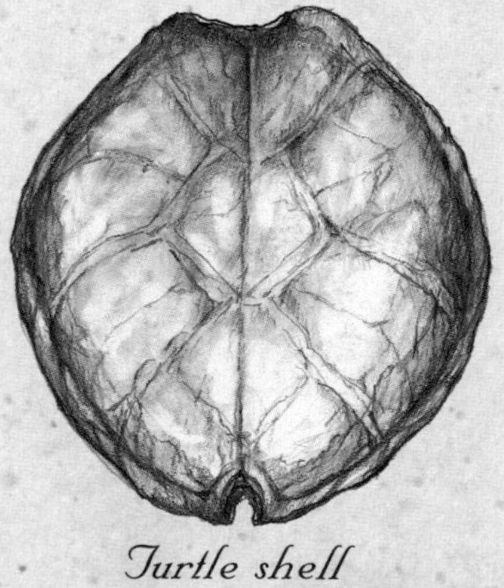

Turtle shell
Almost all the families of turtles alive today, from small box to giant sea turtles, existed in prehistoric times.

With winter approaching, Earl Douglass was breaking up camp, when William Holland arrived for a visit.

While working in the field, Douglass always kept detailed notes about his daily explorations for future reference. As the two men discussed the geological observations in the notebook entries, the museum director—an amateur collector—suggested a final fossil-hunting expedition for the season.

They set out by mule team and wagon.

Following the ridge of Dead Man's Bench, they headed north, bound for an area where John Wesley Powell, the famous explorer, wrote of finding fossil evidence of "reptilian remains" in 1871, during his second trip down the Green River to the Grand Canyon. After two days of traveling through sage-covered hills and cedar forests, they emerged above a series of deep carved gullies.

The two men immediately recognized the gully walls as Jurassic strata, a likely sign that bone beds lay below. Going off in opposite directions—as bone hunters do—they began to search for fossils.

Each carried a gun to fire as a signal should he come upon something of interest.

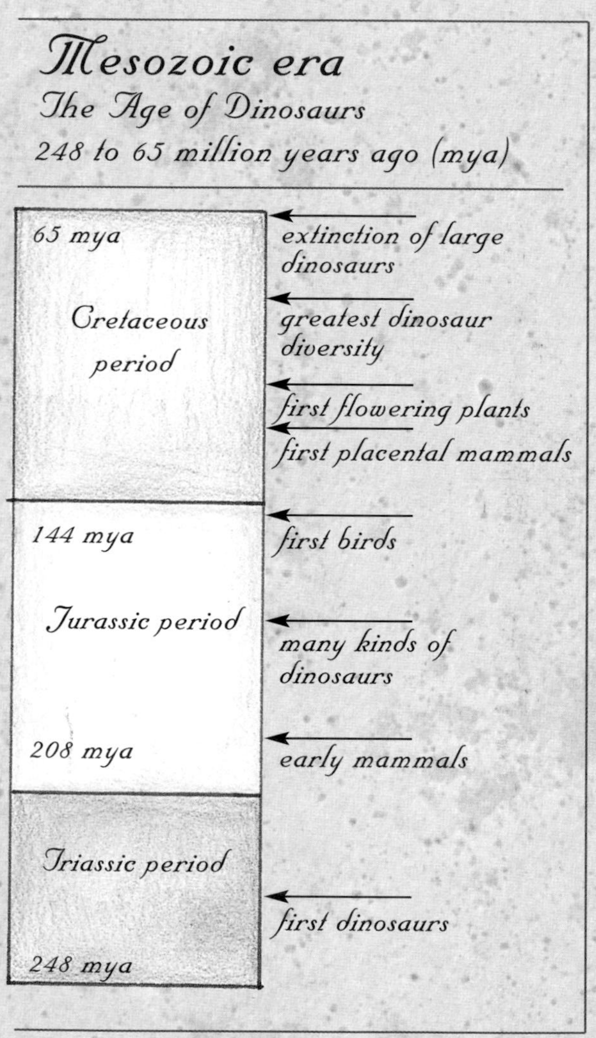

Dr. Holland heard a shot and headed down in its direction.

Earl Douglass was far below, in a narrow ravine. Beside him lay a gigantic thighbone—nearly six feet long.

Both men examined the dinosaur bone that Douglass identified as belonging to a *Diplodocus*. Then they discussed its puzzling location.

Bones are usually found in the layers of sedimentary rock. This bone lay fully exposed, alone, on the sandy floor of a dry ravine. How long had it been bleaching in the sun, and from where in the Jurassic strata had it washed down? If its origin could be found, Douglass thought it likely that he would find more dinosaur bones, and perhaps even whole skeletons.

He wouldn't know until he "walked out" the rock formation—a term bone hunters use for systematically searching an area by following a particular layer of rock. But there was no time.

Nor could the bone be moved for further study, because of its weight and location.

Douglass marked the spot as a starting place, certain of only two things—that there was something big in the Uinta Basin, and that he would be back to continue searching.

> *I came up to him standing beside the weathered-out femur . . . as clean and perfect as if it had been worked out from the matrix in a laboratory.*
>
> —William Holland

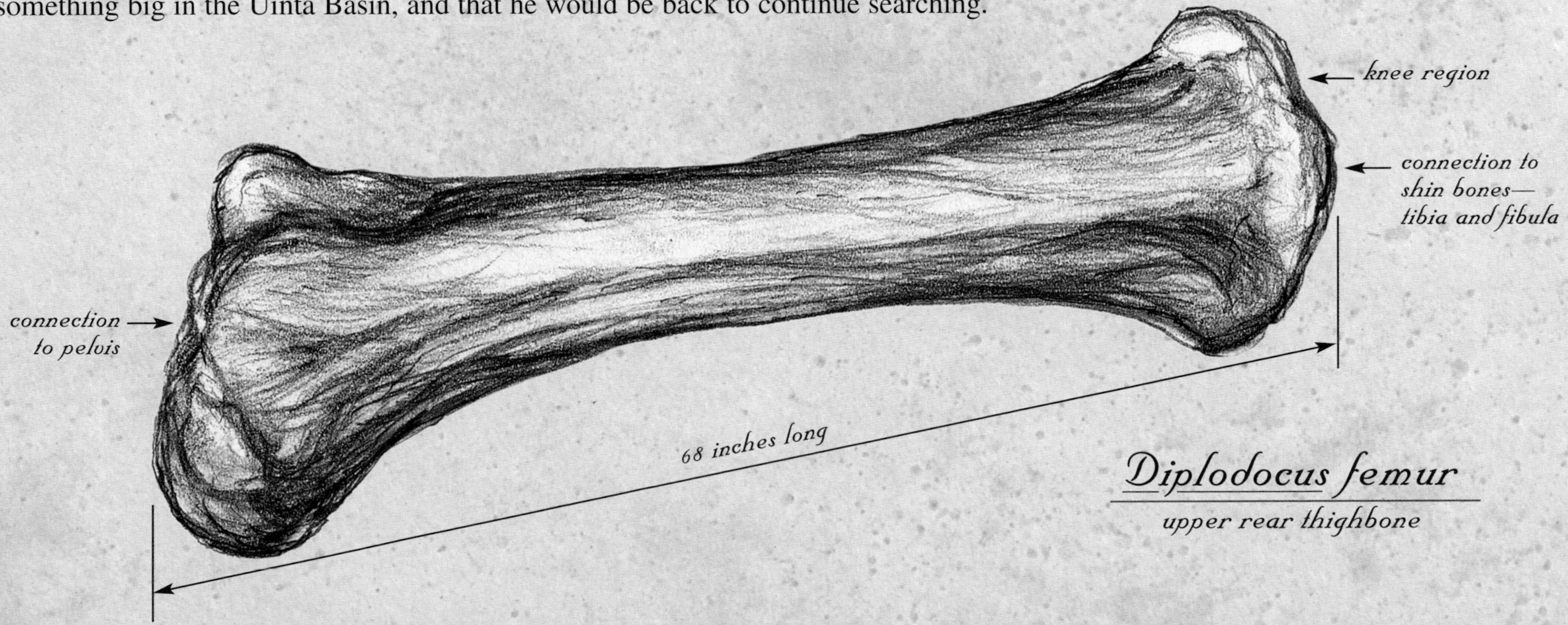

Diplodocus femur

upper rear thighbone

Jurassic strata
near the Green River in the Uinta Basin

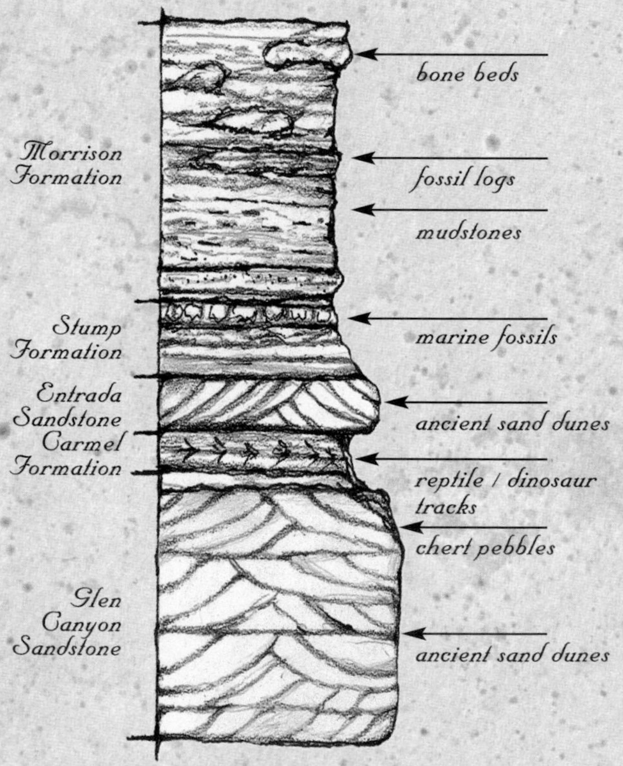

In the early spring of 1909, Earl Douglass returned to the same location in Utah. He began his quest for dinosaur-bearing strata hopefully.

Accompanying him on the bone hunt was George "Dad" Goodrich, an elderly local resident with an interest in fossils.

Day after day and week after week, all through spring and into the heat of summer, they walked the outcrops looking for signs of bones.

They followed the drainages made by snowmelt runoff, where newly exposed bone is often spotted weathering out. They walked up and down, and in and out of gullies and canyons. They scrambled and stumbled over rocks, and sometimes fell. But all they found were small bone fragments. None were even worth keeping.

As Douglass wrote in his field notes: *Went out prospecting again coming out of the gulch I went in the day before. Found Dinosaur bones but nothing good. Saw broken remains of a little fellow. Once in awhile one can get a good limb bone here and I do not doubt that there are good specimens to be had but they don't appear to be very common.*

Douglass had begun to lose all hope of finding something big.

On the morning of August 17, 1909, Earl Douglass and "Dad" Goodrich were scouting for bones near Split Mountain, a canyon cut by the rushing Green River.

Douglass was walking along a knobby ridge when a flash of something bright in the sharply tilted sandstone caught his eye. Exposed bone! He fired his gun to signal, and bolted up the slope.

Douglass wrote: *At last in the top of the ledge where the softer overlying (sandstone) beds form a divide—a kind of saddle I saw eight of the tail bones of a Brontosaurus in exact position. It was a beautiful sight. Part of the ledge had weathered away and several of the vertebra had weathered out and the beautifully petrified centra lay on the ground.*

If the eight vertebrae were still together, perhaps the rest of the tailbones were there as well. His heart pounded with anticipation as he began to chip into the sandstone. Slowly, one tailbone after another was revealed.

With mounting excitement, Douglass and Goodrich probed and chipped into the rock layer, day after day, until finally almost the entire dinosaur was uncovered.

It was the skeleton of an *Apatosaurus* (formerly called *Brontosaurus*)—more than seventy feet long. *Apatosaurus* was one of the largest animals ever to walk the earth.

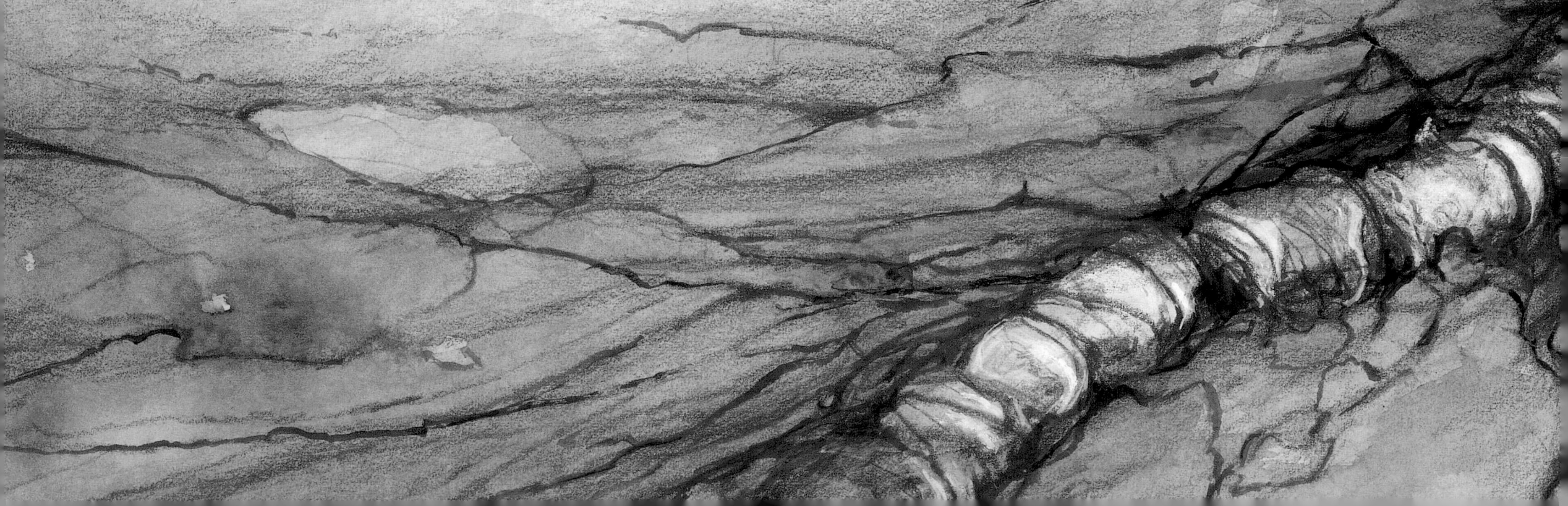

After the discovery, Earl Douglass remained in Utah, and the dinosaur mountain became his life's work. With funding from the Carnegie Museum, he set up what would become known as the Carnegie Quarry.

Planning a major excavation was a daunting task in so isolated and harsh a place, where winter comes early and lasts for many months. Using a sheepherder's wagon as his office, Douglass immediately went to work—ordering supplies, hiring a small crew, and surveying and mapping the fossil-bearing bed.

All the equipment needed to operate a quarry had to be shipped by rail to the closest junction, more than thirty miles away by mountain roads. He enlisted men from the surrounding ranches, with tractors and wagons and teams of horses, to cut a road up the steep mountain and haul supplies to the bone-digging site.

Douglass's wife, Pearl, and one-year-old son, Gawin, joined him in the Utah wilderness at the end of September. The family lived in canvas-covered lean-to structures—one for cooking, another for sleeping, and a third for storage—throughout their first bitterly cold, snowy winter.

We usually get up . . . near six o'clock. I go and quickly start the fires. Pearl gets up and usually Gawin wakes up so she has to dress him. I help get breakfast which consists of usually three or four of the following. Pork, Ham, Bacon, Eggs, Hot Biscuits, Johnny Cake, Corn Fritters, Cream of Wheat, sometimes pancakes, Coffee . . .

We all went up to the diggings in the forenoon. Moved a good deal of dirt . . .

Very cold. We think it is about down to −40°. Clear. I did not suffer much working. A fellow has to look out for his ears, nose, and toes.

—Earl Douglass

Digging getting more interesting. Hate to quit at noon and night . . . The stratum is full of bones . . . Bones are going diagonally through cliff. Looks like a delta deposit and the current to east . . .

Getting ready to shoot behind No. 1. Plastered ends of tail bones and a specimen a little distance away which I had thought might be tail . . . It does look as if we are to get an almost complete skeleton . . .

Of all things I must not injure the specimen by carelessness or want of skill.

—Earl Douglass

When spring arrived at last, the Douglass family began construction of a small house, on land they would homestead, adjacent to the quarry.

And Earl Douglass and his crew were ready to start digging.

Digging dinosaurs was hard, slow work—and it was dangerous.

It had been possible to reveal the *Apatosaurus* skeleton because it was already near the surface. But it was quite another problem to remove the bones from their rocky tomb. Or to find the bones of other dinosaurs that were buried deeper in the mountain.

The entire fossil-bearing rock layer was behind a steeply slanted sandstone wall. A trench had to be dug down from the top to reach the bone beds.

First the crew removed layers of clay and shale with pickaxes and shovels. Then, because the heavy sandstone that held the bones was so hard, they blasted the mountainside with dynamite charges.

After the blasting, holes were drilled into the wall, where wedges were inserted, then sledgehammered until the sandstone broke apart.

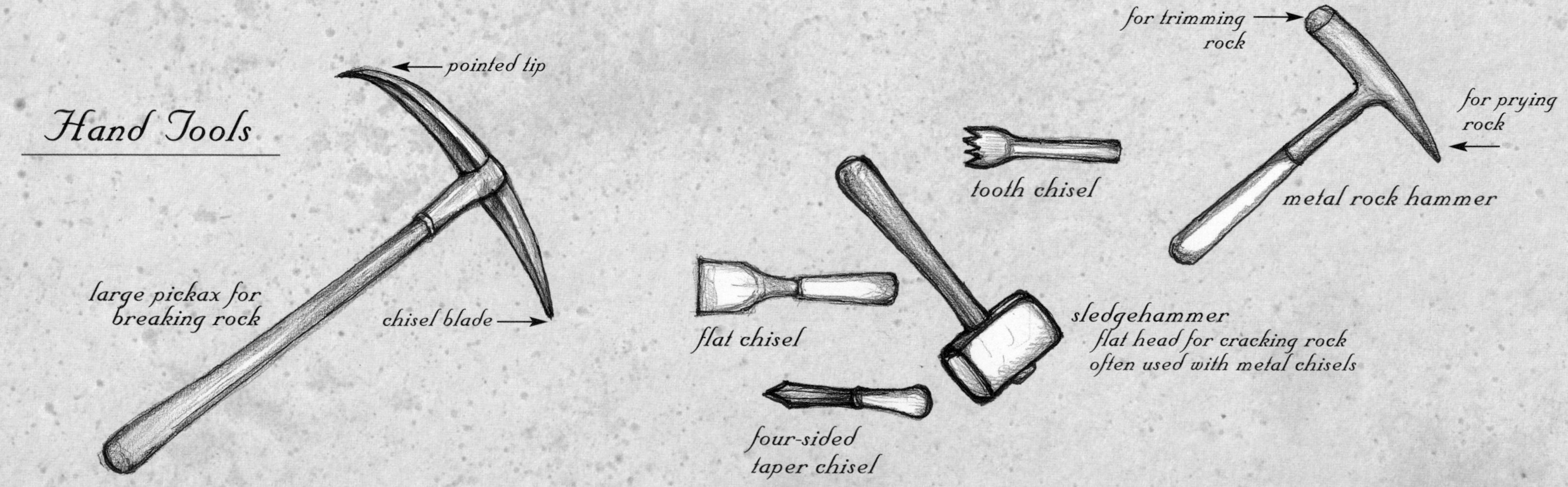

TNT

Femur
15 vert
14 vert
13 vert
Blk
388

When the crew finally reached a skeleton, small chisels and light hammers were used to cut away the rock close to the fragile bones. They were then covered with thin paper, and wrapped in burlap strips that were dipped in plaster. The plaster casts, called jackets, protected the bones from damage during removal from the rock, and later during transport to the museum.

During the Bone Wars, both Cope and Marsh had made mistakes in their haste for glory. When assembling the dinosaurs, sometimes they confused bones, attaching the wrong head to a skeleton, or erring on the posture.

Earl Douglass was determined that such mistakes would not happen with the bones from the Carnegie Quarry. Each plaster jacket was immediately labeled and the bone assigned a number.

Painting a grid directly on the bone-bearing layer, he diagrammed the numbered bones in their original positions, then copied all the information to a smaller chart that would accompany the bones to the museum.

The bones were packed in strong wooden crates for the long journey east, by railroad, to Pennsylvania. It took four years to dig out, transport, and mount the skeleton of the *Apatosaurus louisae* (named for Andrew Carnegie's wife, Louise) at the museum.

It requires long, slow, painstaking work to prepare dinosaur bones for exhibition. After the plaster jackets are carefully sawed off the bones, all the surrounding rock is delicately scraped away, sometimes using dental tools. Real bones are often too fragile to display. Each bone is cast in a mold to make an exact copy. The replica—made of plaster or plastic—is then painted to look like bone. Once the proper posture for the dinosaur is decided, the skeleton is assembled on a metal framework called an armature.

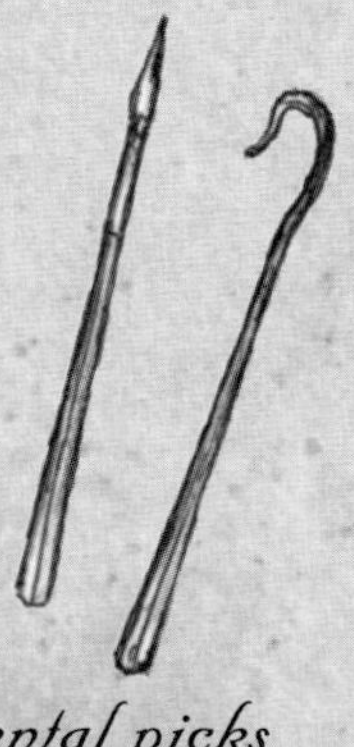
dental picks

small whisk broom
for removing loose dirt

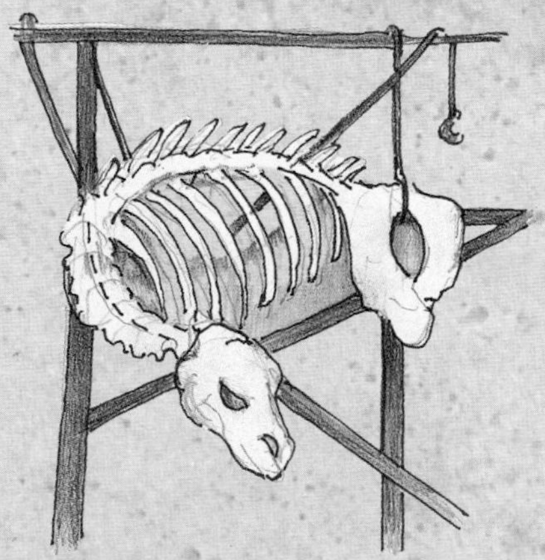
dinosaur on armature

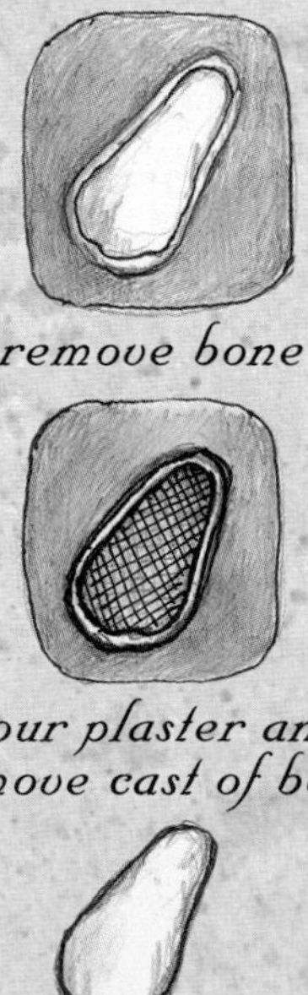

Yesterday . . . was a day which we hope will be worthy to be remembered. It was the day in which we discovered one of the two great things for which we are searching . . . a skull! . . .

We started the practice too of having a turkey and a skull feast whenever we found a skull . . .

Dreamed the greater part of the night of working on Diplodocus skull . . . I would awake and get up then go to bed and dream it over and over . . .

We are still busily pecking away at the quarry . . .

The space which contains the bones is not so great but they are so piled on one another and interlocked that it is mostly a matter of continual pecking away with small tools . . . We have . . . the lower jaw of Brontosaurus, a skull associated with the neck of Diplodocus (the first time such a thing has been known) . . . And almost every day there are surprises or something new or unknown coming to light.

—Earl Douglass

Meanwhile, Earl Douglass kept digging.

The excavation went further down and deeper into the mountain. And year after year, the mountain revealed more treasures. More and more bones were removed from the sandstone. Many were nearly complete dinosaur skeletons. Sometimes they were piled one on top of another. Often bones of different dinosaurs were mixed together, carried downstream, Douglass believed, along an ancient river channel to this final resting place.

Work went along, productive and undisturbed, until more people moved into the area. What had been vast unpopulated rangeland surrounding the quarry was now being settled. There were instances of trespassing and vandalism—even theft of bones.

Fearful that precious fossils, as yet undiscovered, would be disturbed, Douglass filed a mining claim to protect the area.

But the mining office refused his claim, saying that bones are not minerals.

When that failed, he wrote letters to government officials pleading for federal protection of the nearby land and quarry.

Finally, President Woodrow Wilson learned of the problem. On October 4, 1915, he proclaimed 80 acres surrounding the excavation as Dinosaur National Monument.

Four years later, Andrew Carnegie died. With their benefactor gone, the museum could no longer afford to support the entire operation of the quarry. A small grant provided by the University of Utah helped keep it open.

Though unpaid, Earl Douglass continued to dig until the quarry closed in 1924.

By the time he left, penniless and in poor health, most of the east and west sides of the quarry had been stripped, and about 350 tons of fossil material had been shipped to the Carnegie and other museums.

The site would prove to be the most productive Jurassic-age quarry in the United States.

Ten different species of Jurassic dinosaurs were excavated. These include the plant-eating sauropods *Apatosaurus* (formerly known as *Brontosaurus*), *Barosaurus*, *Camarasaurus*, and *Diplodocus*, plant-eating ornithopods *Camptosaurus* and *Dryosaurus*, the plated *Stegosaurus*, and meat-eating theropods *Allosaurus*, *Ceratosaurus*, and *Ornitholestes*.

Earl Douglass had indeed found something big.

Here is one of the greatest curiosities in the world—a burying ground of the huge prehistoric beasts of a long distant age. It is a combination of fortunate circumstances that they have been buried, preserved and again unveiled to us . . .

The now famous dinosaur quarry like many other such finds of the kind might long have remained undiscovered had not a few bones of the tail of one dinosaur been partly exposed on the face of a ledge of sandstone . . .

The view we are now getting of the past by discovery of fossil animals and plants makes the present world ever new to us . . . a little window for a world of the imagination.

—Earl Douglass

After the quarry closed, Earl Douglass worked for the University of Utah, and moved to Salt Lake City. But he never lost his love for the dinosaur mountain. He was often seen driving the quarry road in his Model T Ford.

The Jurassic Dinosaurs of the Dinosaur National Monument Quarry

Apatosaurus “Deceptive lizard”

Named by Othniel Marsh in 1877, then named *Brontosaurus* in 1879. Renamed *Apatosaurus* in the 1970s, when the skull description was corrected. Weighed about 34 tons, and measured 75 feet long. It had short, sharp teeth for stripping leaves off branches. The only known skull of this giant sauropod was found at the quarry.

Barosaurus “Heavy lizard”

Named by Othniel Marsh in 1890. Discovered in South Dakota. Weighed about 25 tons, and measured 80 feet long. It was among the longest of the plant-eating sauropods, with a 30-foot neck that could reach into treetops.

Camarasaurus “Chamber lizard”

Named by Edward Drinker Cope in 1877. Discovered at Garden Park, Colorado. Two species are known, one large and one small. The small 17-foot juvenile excavated from the quarry is the most complete sauropod skeleton ever found.

Diplodocus “Double beam”

Named by Othniel Marsh in 1878. It is among the longest of the known sauropods. An 84-foot skeleton found in Como Bluff, Wyoming, was named for Andrew Carnegie, who bought it for his dinosaur hall in 1899. Nicknamed “Dippy,” it is still on exhibit.

Stegosaurus “Plated lizard”

Named by Othniel Marsh in 1877. Discovered in Morrison, Colorado. It was an armored, slow-moving grazer whose plates are thought by some paleontologists to have controlled body heat. Very common at the quarry—their skeletons were often mixed in among sauropod bones.

Camptosaurus "Bent lizard"

Named by Othniel Marsh in 1885. Discovered at Como Bluff, Wyoming. A plant-eating ornithopod. It measured about 15 feet long, weighed about a ton, and could walk on two or four legs.

Dryosaurus "Oak lizard"

Named by Othniel Marsh in 1894. Also discovered at Como Bluff. A small, fast plant eater that ran on its two hind legs, it was only 6 feet long.

Allosaurus "Other lizard"

Named by Othniel Marsh in 1877. First found in Colorado. A fierce theropod with powerful jaws and long teeth, it attacked even the giant plant eaters. Two skeletons, one with a nearly perfect skull, were excavated from the quarry.

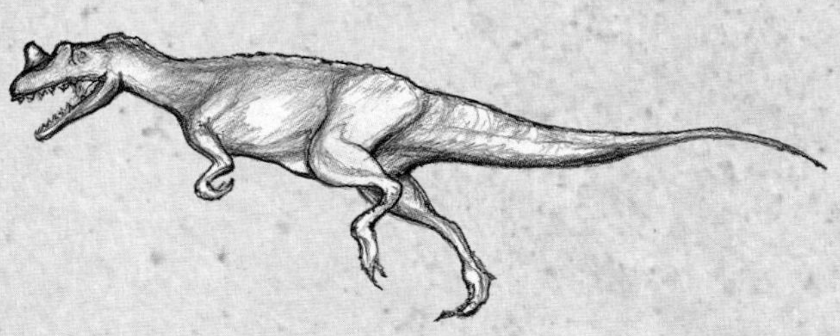

Ceratosaurus "Horned lizard"

Named by Othniel Marsh in 1884. Discovered at Garden Park, Colorado. A powerful horned theropod that walked on two legs and preyed on smaller dinosaurs.

Ornitholestes "Bird robber"

Named by paleontologist Henry Osborn in 1903. Discovered in Wyoming. A speedy theropod with a long tail, it hunted small reptiles. Formerly believed to have a small horn, but recent skull discoveries have shown this is not true.

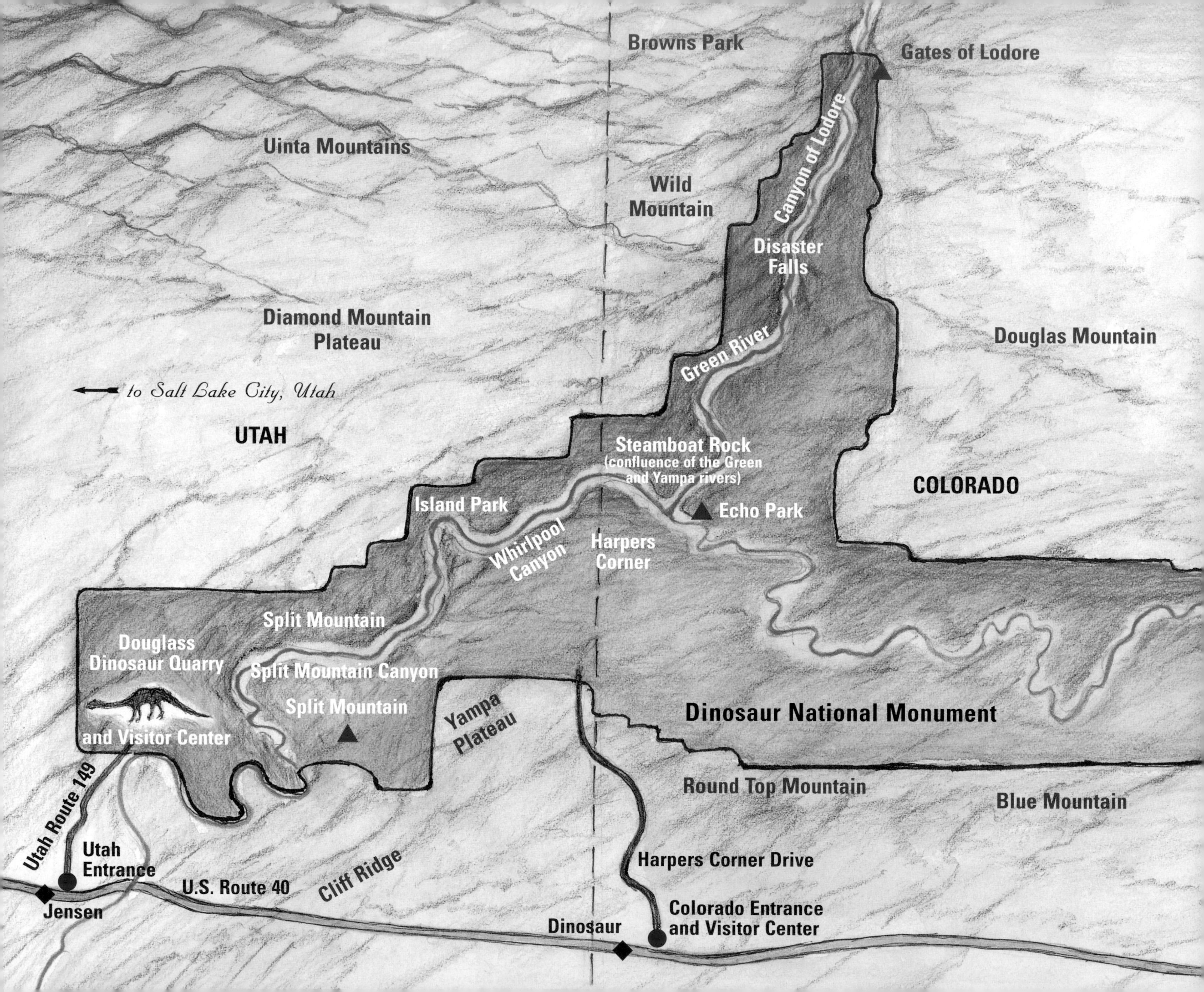
Browns Park
Gates of Lodore
Uinta Mountains
Wild Mountain
Canyon of Lodore
Disaster Falls
Diamond Mountain Plateau
Douglas Mountain
Green River
to Salt Lake City, Utah
UTAH
Steamboat Rock
(confluence of the Green and Yampa rivers)
COLORADO
Island Park
Echo Park
Whirlpool Canyon
Harpers Corner
Split Mountain
Douglass Dinosaur Quarry
Split Mountain Canyon
Split Mountain
and Visitor Center
Yampa Plateau
Dinosaur National Monument
Round Top Mountain
Blue Mountain
Utah Route 149
Utah Entrance
Harpers Corner Drive
Cliff Ridge
U.S. Route 40
Jensen
Colorado Entrance and Visitor Center
Dinosaur

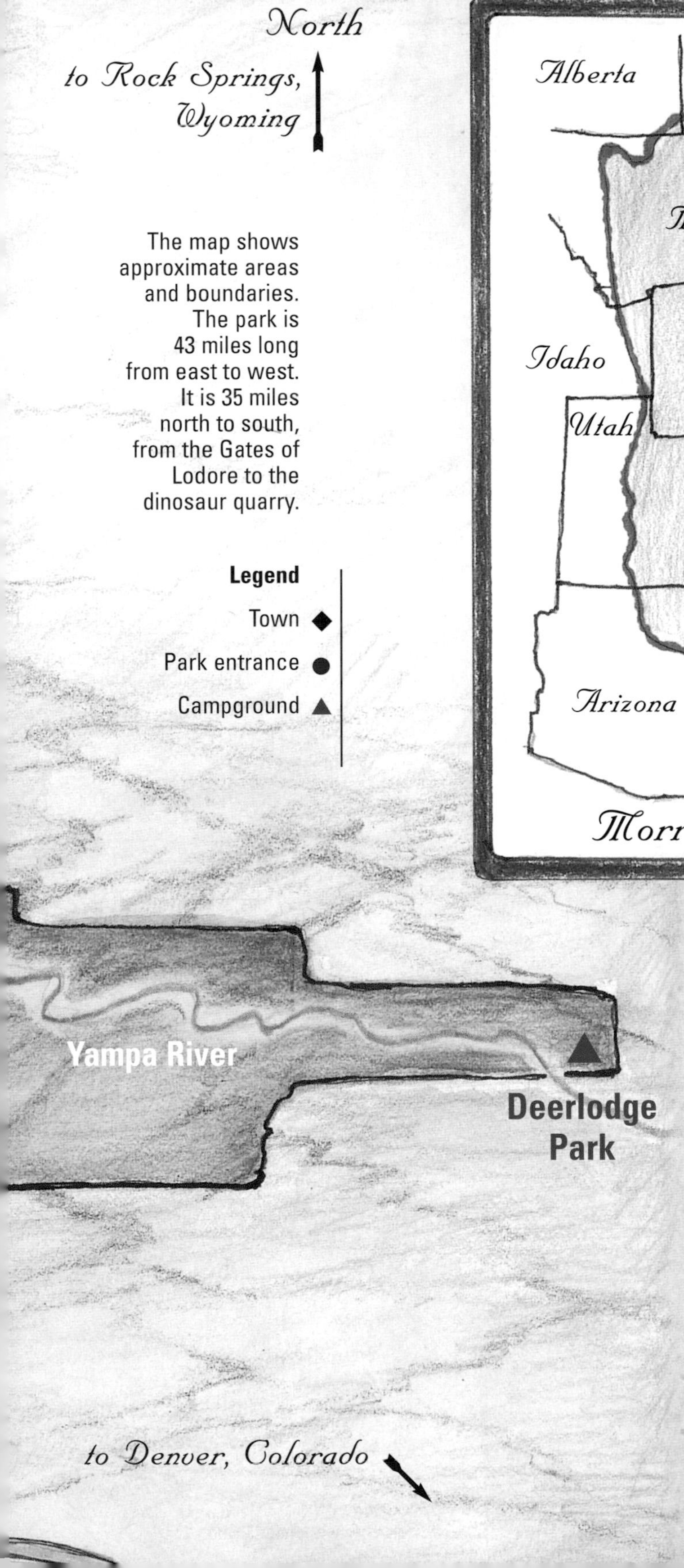

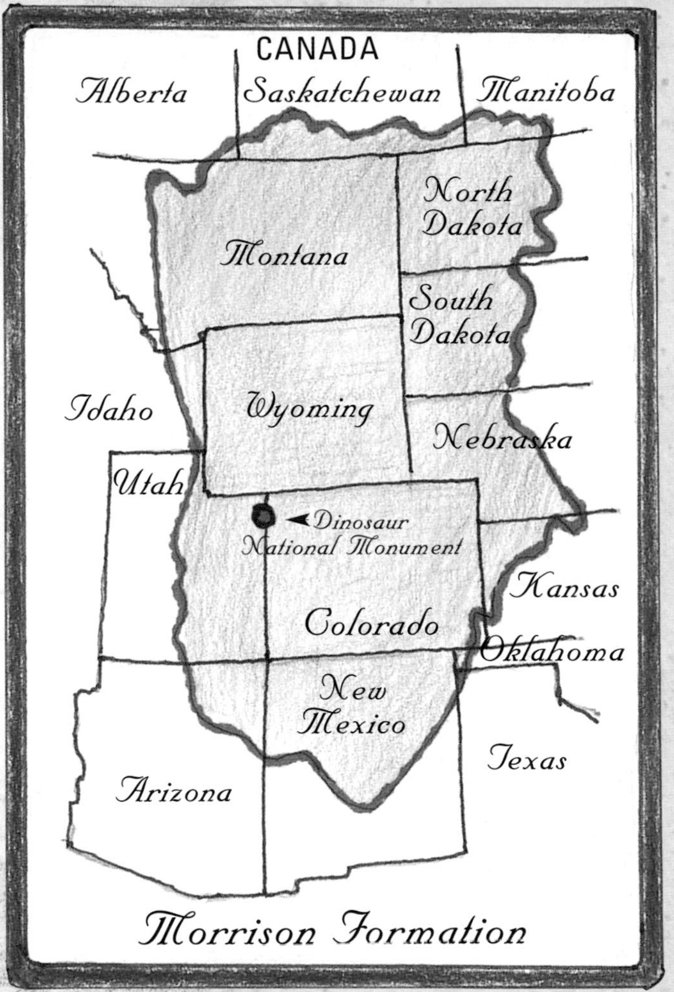

With trained men and money we might make one of the great exhibits of the world and perhaps we will be permitted to do it. We may be dreaming and that is all right.
—Earl Douglass

Dinosaur National Monument

Dinosaur National Monument was enlarged to 210,000 acres in 1938. Now stretching from Utah across to northwestern Colorado, it both protects and gives public access to a vast and varied landscape that is rich in plant and animal life.

In 1915, when President Wilson first created Dinosaur National Monument, Earl Douglass wrote in his diary that he wished someday the quarry would be made into an exhibit for the public.

"I hope that the Government, for the benefit of science and the people, will uncover a large area, leave the bones and skeletons in relief and house them in. It would make one of the most astounding and instructive sights imaginable," Douglass wrote to the Smithsonian Institution in Washington, D.C., in 1923.

It took more than thirty years until that wish was realized.

In 1958, the National Park Service completed construction of a huge glass building that enclosed the rock face where Douglass made his first discovery. "The Wall," as it became known to many thousands of awestruck visitors, reveals more than fifteen hundred tangled bones—exactly as they were deposited in the Jurassic age.

The quarry, originally named for Andrew Carnegie, is now called the Douglass Quarry, in honor of the man who discovered and treasured it.

Author's Note

The question that many people who visit the Douglass Quarry ask is: How did so many dinosaurs end up in one place?

No one is certain of the answer. But geological evidence tells us that in the Jurassic period an enormous flat plain existed in what is now the western United States. A wide river flowed through the area, and many kinds of dinosaurs lived all along its lush, green banks.

Earl Douglass believed the site of the quarry had once been a sandbar in the river. As animals died, their bodies would have been carried downstream, eventually becoming lodged in this shallow place. Over the ages, their bones were buried deeper and deeper in layers of sand and mud that eventually hardened into rock. As the earth's plates shifted, the rocks rose up to form mountains.

Standing at the quarry, atop a bare mountain, it is hard to believe that the area could once have been a river channel, or that such a landscape ever existed here. But the earth is constantly changing.

In 2006, the National Park Service closed the Quarry Visitor Center because of movement in the rock under the foundation of the building. A new building to house the famous bone wall has recently been scheduled for construction, with hopes that it will open to the public in late spring 2011.

Earl Douglass

(1862–1931)

Earl Douglass was born on October 23, 1862, in the small town of Medford in southern Minnesota. From an early age, he was fascinated by the natural world, and he spent his boyhood reading about earth sciences. His interest in plants led him to study botany at the South Dakota Agriculture College.

While working for the Missouri Botanical Gardens, he took courses at Washington University in St. Louis, and his scientific interest shifted to geology and mammal fossils.

For six years, he taught school for a living while he conducted independent fossil explorations and attended the University of Montana, earning a Master of Science degree in geology. In western Montana, he found several extinct mammals that were unknown to science. On the basis of these discoveries, he was awarded a fellowship from Princeton University in New Jersey, where he studied geology, paleontology, and anatomy.

In 1902, the Carnegie Museum in Pittsburgh hired Douglass as a fossil expert, and purchased his collection of extinct mammal fossils. Over the next several years, he divided his time between work at the museum and geological expeditions to the western United States, including a trip to Utah in 1907. In 1908 and 1909, he explored the Uinta Basin of northeastern Utah in search of dinosaur remains for the museum. On August 17, 1909, he discovered the skeleton of an *Apatosaurus*.

Andrew Carnegie

(1835–1919)

Andrew Carnegie was born in Scotland. His family moved to America in 1848 and settled in what is now Pittsburgh, Pennsylvania, where his formal education ended and he began to work in a textile mill as a bobbin boy at the age of thirteen. A self-made man, Carnegie eventually became a multimillionaire through a series of investments in railroads, oil, and steel. When he sold his Carnegie Steel Company for $480 million and retired in 1901, he was the richest man in the world. Though he never paid his employees well, Carnegie's motto was "the man who dies thus rich dies disgraced," and he donated much of his money for the social good. He established universities and museums, and funded research, education, and the promotion of world peace. He endowed the Teachers' Pension Fund for ten million dollars, and built more than twenty-five hundred libraries around the world. By the time he died in 1919, Carnegie had given away ninety percent of his fortune.

Glossary

bone bed A layer of rock that contains many fossils.

centra The bones in the center of the vertebrae that attach one to the other.

dinosaur Any of an extinct group of reptiles that walked with their legs held directly under their bodies.

extinct A term used to describe animals or plants that have died out.

formation A sequence of rock layers that can be traced across a large area.

fossil A remnant or the remains of an ancient plant or animal that has been preserved in rock.

geology The study of rocks and the history of the earth, including how it was formed and how it changed.

marl A mixture of clay, sand, and limestone (calcite).

ornithopods A group of bird-hipped dinosaurs.

outcrop The part of a rock formation that is exposed on the surface of the ground.

paleontology The study of the life of past geologic periods.

sandstone A sedimentary rock typically made of cemented sand and rock debris.

sauropods A group of giant, long-necked, lizard-hipped dinosaurs.

sedimentary rock Rock formed from deposits of sand, mud, and clay.

stratum A single layer of sedimentary rock.

theropods Meat eaters forming another group of lizard-hipped dinosaurs.

Bibliography

Barrett, Paul. *National Geographic Dinosaurs*. Illustrated by Raul Martin. Washington, D.C.: National Geographic Society, 2001.

Colbert, Edwin H. *The Great Dinosaur Hunters and Their Discoveries*. Mineola, N.Y.: Dover Publications, 1984.

Hagood, Allen, and Linda West. *Dinosaur: The Story Behind the Scenery*. Las Vegas, Nev.: KC Publications, 1999.

Horner, Jack. *Digging Up Dinosaurs*. Helena, Mont.: Farcountry Press, 2007.

Leach, Nicky. *The National Parks of Utah: A Journey to the Colorado Plateau*. Mariposa, Calif.: Sierra Press, 2002.

Rea, Tom. *Bone Wars: The Excavation and Celebrity of Andrew Carnegie's Dinosaur*. Pittsburgh, Pa.: University of Pittsburgh Press, 2001.

Stegner, Wallace. *Mormon Country*. Lincoln, Neb.: University of Nebraska Press, 2003.

Weishampel, David B., and Nadine M. White, eds. *The Dinosaur Papers: 1676–1906*. Washington, D.C.: Smithsonian Books, 2003.

For Karen and Francisco, who introduced me to the wonders of the western slope —D.K.R.

Permission granted to quote from the Earl Douglass Collection, Ms 196, University of Utah Library. My thanks to the Carnegie Museum of Natural History for historical photographs, to the National Park Service for photographs and information about Dinosaur National Park, and to Lowell Dingus, Research Associate, Division of Paleontology, American Museum of Natural History, for his critical help in making this book.

Distributed in Canada by D&M Publishers, Inc.
Color separations by Chroma Graphics PTE Ltd.
Printed in October 2009 in China by Macmillan Production (Asia) Ltd., Kwun Tong, Kowloon, Hong Kong
(Supplier code: 10)
Designed by Barbara Grzeslo
First edition, 2010
1 3 5 7 9 10 8 6 4 2

www.fsgkidsbooks.com

Library of Congress Cataloging-in-Publication Data
Ray, Deborah Kogan, date.
Dinosaur mountain : digging into the Jurassic age / Deborah Kogan Ray.
p. cm.
ISBN: 978-0-374-31789-8
1. Dinosaur National Monument (Colo. and Utah)—History—Juvenile literature. 2. Dinosaurs—Colorado—Juvenile literature. 3. Dinosaurs—Utah—Juvenile literature. 4. Paleontology—Colorado—Juvenile literature. 5. Paleontology—Utah—Juvenile literature. I. Title.
QE861.8.C6R39 2010
567.90973—dc22

2008027877

Photograph of Earl Douglass courtesy of the Special Collections Department, J. Willard Marriott Library, University of Utah.

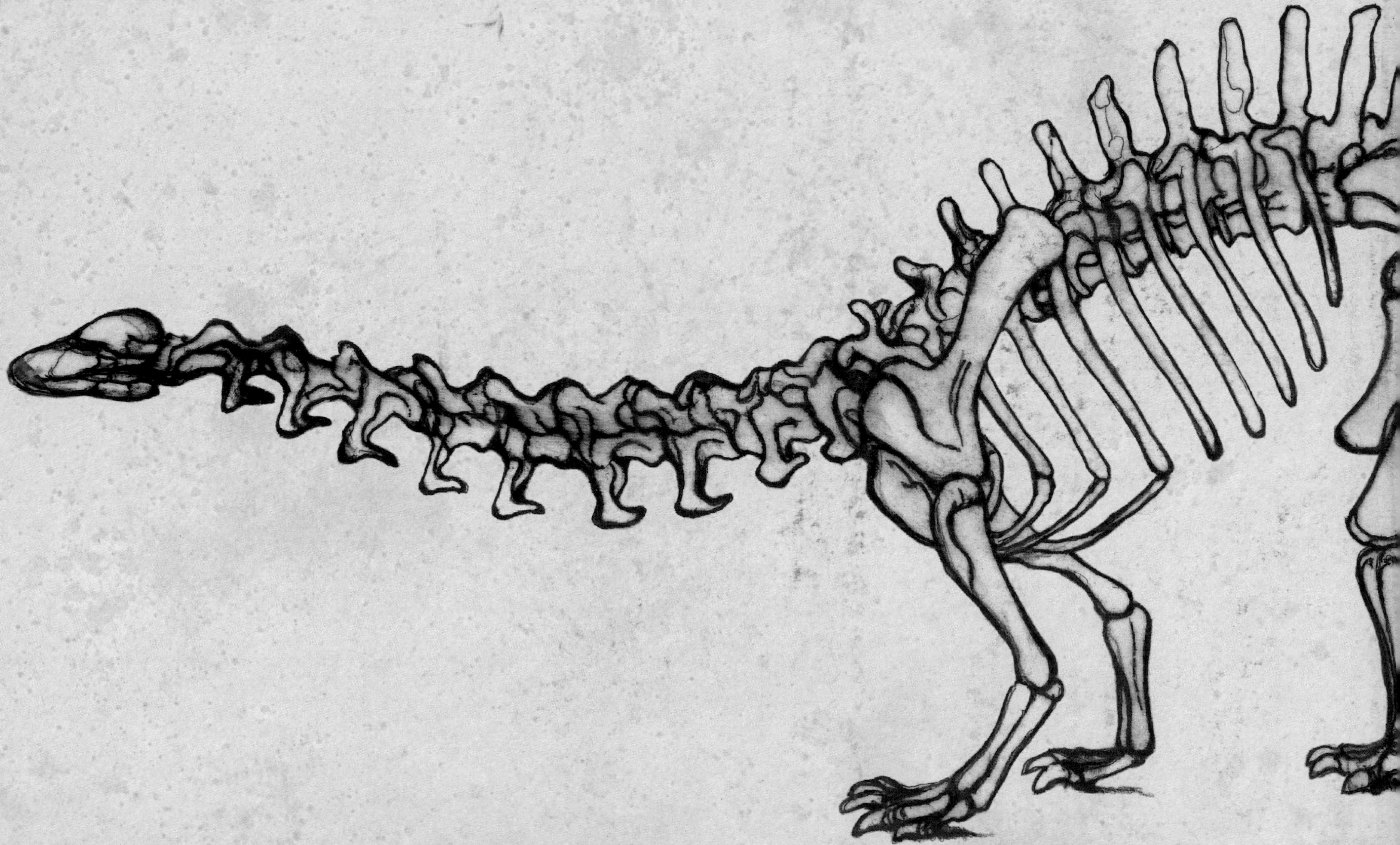

Skeleton of *Apatosaurus excelsus* (*Brontosaurus excelsus*) copied from an 1883 drawing by O. C. Marsh